F1:

A History of Formula One Racing

By Frank Foster

BookCaps™ Study Guides
www.bookcaps.com

Table of Contents

ABOUT HISTORYCAPS

HistoryCaps is an imprint of BookCaps™ Study Guides. With each book, a brief period of history is recapped. We publish a wide array of topics (from baseball and music to science and philosophy), so check our growing catalogue regularly (www.book-caps.com) to see our newest books.

INTRODUCTION

For as long as there have been automobiles, there have been courageous men and women with nerves of steel, willing to risk life and limb to race them. The heart pounding adrenaline rush that engulfed men like Guiseppe Farina, Juan Manuel Fangio, Jack Brabham and Sterling Moss. Pioneers of the motor sport which has roots that run deep through European culture. And the women, the little known names of females drivers who gave their all to race wheel to wheel with their male counterparts: Helle

Nice, Desiree Wilson, Giovanna Amati and Lella Lombardi.

Only a decade after the creation of the first automobile, in 1884, grand prix racing was born in Europe. Before WWII, the sport was a popular past time in Europe featuring open wheeled Bugatti's and races like the Donington Grand Prix. The thrills were felt by spectators as well as drivers and in particular by one Adolph Hitler. Hitler used grand prix racing as a form of his propaganda, having his people race cars, and even creating a type of formula for racing. With the onset of the war, grand prix racing was put on hold.

During the war, Britain and the allies built several airfields and bases. One such base was Silverstone Airfield, home to the 17th division training base built on the outskirts of the small country village of Silverstone in the county of Northamptonshire England. From the pre-war era of Hitlers propaganda racing, to the new, post war era of new, young drivers, and make-shift tracks made from those old air base runways, Formula One's roots were firmly planted in European soil.

At the turn of the 20th century, governing boards were created to oversee this dangerous sport. The governing board of all forms of automobile racing

since 1904, the Formulae Du International L'automobile (FIA) began discussing incorporation of
Formula One rules and regulations after the war in
1946. They finalized in 1947.

Throughout the years, the advances in technology
and safety have emerged with both cars and tracks,
despite the rivalries of the builders and the scan-
dals along the way. Many of the changes have been
sparked by the saddening deaths of illustrious men
in the sport like Lorenzo Bandini from Italy who
died in 1967 at the Monaco Grand Prix; Jean Berha
from France who died in 1959 at Avus; Stephan
Belloff, from Germany who died in 1985 at Spa,
which is a track well known for taking lives; and
Lucien Bianchi an Italian from Belgium. Lucien
died at LeMans in 1969. Sadly, this list is much
longer. The need to go faster, the drive to be the
best, fosters a mentality that some people may find
hard to understand. Yet for those whose lives are
centered around this sport, there is no greater feeling than to be the first to the checkered flag.

CHAPTER 1: THE EARLY YEARS

Grand Prix racing has been around for over 100 years. A decade after the first car was made, the first race took place in France, in 1894. There were 21 drivers taking part in this European road race from Paris to Rouen. Over eighty miles of public roads, these fearless driver with their savvy mechanics in the passenger seat beside them, raced across the country side, stopping only for lunch or to repair a broken car, all for the prize winnings of 5000 francs.

As the years went on France, was the country to embrace road racing. This could be seen with the creation of the Automobile Club du France (ACF) in 1896. Britain and Germany had banned the dangerous sport where drivers and mechanics created cars to win races. Adaptations for speed could be seen as early as 1897. These adaptations meant nonessential parts of the car were removed, and this proved to be extremely dangerous because what some considered essential, others considered nonessential.

In America, in 1911, the absolute first race at Indianapolis took place as Americans showed their interest in the mainly European sport. This track is one of only two tracks used by current Formula One racing in America, the other being Watkins Glen.

Before World War 1, grand prix racing was a popular European sport, amongst spectators and drivers alike. This also included the likes of Adolf Hitler, who in the 1930's saw racing as a way of spreading his propaganda by having drivers of his choosing run races in his cars. It was also Germany that created the first Formula, or set of rules to run the races and one of the reasons for Germany's domination in the sport at that time. There were also talks within the world of Grand Prix regarding formula racing – races with predetermined rules such as Germany had - to make them for all races across the board. This did not get off the ground as the war broke out in Europe and all racing stopped.

During the war, many army and air force bases sprung up on the European and British countryside. One such base was the Silverstone air base in Britain built in 1943 outside of the small village with the same name in the county of Northamptonshire. It consisted of two bitumen runways set at 40 degree angles to one another. The first was an 850 meter runway, the other was 1000 meters. This base was home to the 17th Operational Training Unit where aircrews were trained on flying the Vickers Wellington twin-engine bombers. After the war ended, it became one of many bases to be decommissioned and all but abandoned.

In 1946, talks were back on for the creation of a World Championship to regain the interest of grand prix racing. The Commission Sportive Internationale (CSI), a branch of the Federation International de l'Automobile (FIA) which was the ruling body of racing founded in 1904, and the predecessor of (FISA) looked to the rules and regulations being run by the Formula One cars of Europe, which had only come to fruition themselves. They incorporated those rules to create a World Championship for Grand Prix racing in 1947, a new vision to be the answer to the Motorcycle World Championship created the year before.

On September 1, 1946 Achille Varzi, a pre-war racing star, won the Turin Grand Prix driving a Alpha-Romeo 158 Alfetta. The Alfetta was an Italian made sports car built for Grand Prix racing and quite a popular little car amongst drivers.

That same year, fresh from the war and eager to put his Frazer-Nash to the test, Maurice Geoghegan went to the abandoned airfield near Silverstone, a perfect place to bring his car to speed using the long runways. What he found when he got there was even better than a straight one way run, but a perfect race track using the two runways and the perimeter roads.

A year passed and while out drinking with friends, convinced them that he knew a fantastic place to race. He believed the base to still be utterly abandoned, but much to his surprise, it was not. Farmer, James Wilson Brown, had been leasing the center part of the base for farming. He had free roaming sheep, a piggery and a crop of corn.

On that day, 11 Frazer-Nash's and a Bugatti showed up to the illegal race. During the race, Geoghegan rounded a corner and collided head on with a sheep that had found its way onto the makeshift race track. Both the sheep and the car were totaled, and Maurice Geoghegan had created the name of the race - The Mutton Grand Prix.

That year also saw Formula One born under European rules and regulations. From Spring to Autumn, about twenty races were run in Europe and were dominated by the Italian made Alpha-Romeos. These races followed pre-war rules and regulations which allowed the 4 litre non- supercharged engine cars to race against the 1.5 litre supercharged.

To break it down, there are three formulae of racing, 1, 2, and 3. They were originally referred to as Formula A, B, and 3, and since the final one was never referred to with a letter, they standardized the names as 1, 2, and 3. Each of these formulae regulates based on the size of motor. For Formula 1 original motor sizes were 4500 cc normally aspirated cars and 1500 cc supercharged, Formula 2 had a motor no larger than 2000 cc naturally aspirated or 750 cc supercharged and Formula 3 races only 500 cc horsepower motors.

Looking for championship grade tracks to race their season, the Royal Automobile Club (RAC) heard word of the Mutton Grand Prix and the Silverstone base. Liking what they saw, the club approached the Air Ministry and worked out a lease on the base. Since James Wilson Brown was already familiar with the grounds, the RAC commissioned him to create the race track and gave him two months to do so. Mr. Brown completed this task on time and on October 2, 1948 the 3.67 mile course hosted thousands of fans who came to watch 23 cars race on this newly made track. The winner of the inaugural race was Luigi Villoresi driving a Maserati. He took home L500 for his 1st place winnings.

CHAPTER 2: THE CREATION OF THE WORLD CHAMPIONSHIP

The pre-war heroes like Achille Varzi, Louis Cheron, Rudolph Carracciola, and all time great Tazio Nuvolari had become names of the past. The new names in the world of formula grand prix racing would initally be dominated by the three 'f's of Alpha Romeo drivers. Farina, Fangio, and Fagioli.

Driving the Alfa Romeo 158 supercharged straight 8, these three drivers domiated the first season of the World Championship, finishing first, second, and third respectively.

Some would argue that it is the car that makes the win, others would say its the the driver. All would argree that you can't have one without the other. To be a winner at this sport, fabulous cars need talented drivers to win. With a look at the top ranking cars in the championship, Alfa Romeo was definitly a part of the winning formula with four cars in the top ten.

Despite the sport being in a constant flux of change with designs of cars and tracks, drivers coming and going, the early years were the growing years. The foundation for what we experience today. The 1950's saw many changes, good and bad.

The British Grand Prix at Silverstone was the first race of the World Championship in 1950. It was won by Giuseppe Farina, driving an Alpha Romeo. Farina would also go on to become the first World Champion of Formula One.

The World Championship, put in place as an answer to the World Motorcycle Championship, which had proven to be a big draw for spectators.

The Formula One World Championship was raced in Europe and Britain only, for the first few years. This post-war era saw great changes in the way that grand prix racing was run. What was once a jaunt between towns on the roads, carrying your mechanic with you had turned into a whole new style of strategy and design. Tracks sprouted up in Britain, France and Germany. Tracks like Silverstone with its revamped 2.888 mile circuit; Reims, with an original 4.865 mile circuit that used public roads west of the town of Reims, France; and Nurburgring Nordschleife, a whopping 14.167 miles and considered the 'ultimate red meat circuit', weaved its way throught the majestic Eifel forest with 100 turns. That was the track that challenged both stamina and bravery.

Another track that was part of the championship was the Indianapolis 500. Although this American track saw spectators totaling over 400 000, for the first decade it was not a race that many actual Formula One drivers participated. Most if the grid was usually made up of American oval racing teams. Of the few Formula One drivers who did take part, many considered it as Americans flaunting their peacock plumage.

The first race to be deemed an International Formula One race was run on April 10, 1950. This race was won by Juan Manuel Fangio driving his Maserati to the finish line at the Pau Grand Prix. A driver who opitimized the image of a true race car driver, Fangio influenced future Formula One drivers with his style. He always sat low and relaxed behind the wheel with his arms outstretched, much like how the drivers are today. The following year Fangio grabbed the World Championship.

The 1952 World Championship was won by Alberto Ascari. He drove his Ferrari that year which had to be run under F2 rules due to to lack of support from race organizers. Ascari would clinch the Championship for the next two seasons under regular F1, rules, but his luck would soon run out. In 1955, he was the first driver to ever end up in the harbor at Monaco. He survived the plunge but died in a crash at Monza later that year.

The 1955 race season was one for this history books, and not in a good way. Not all races in a championship season count toward the champioship. About 22 are run in a season, but at the time, only 6 races made up the championship. One of these non-championship races was the Lemans 24 hour race. This race had been run many times in the past, but this particular year would would go down in history as the deadliest race of all time.

Video clips of this crash that took the lives of 83 spectators and driver Pierre Levegh are hard to watch, showing the extent of the tragic carnage that occured that day. The cause of the terrifying crash was a chain reaction that involved drivers Mike Hawthorn, Lance Macklin, Juan Manuel Fangio, and Pierre Levegh.

The cars being driven by those involved in the crash were an Austin-Healy 100, a Jaguar D-type, and two Mercedes 300 SLR's. The SLR's had drum brakes, while the Jaguar of Mike Hawthorn had disk brakes. Disk brakes have a better stopping time than drum brakes, and this turned out to be one of the factors of the crash.

Lap 35 was when the tragedy happened. Mike Hawthorn was in front of Macklin, Levegh and Fangio were quickly approaching the rear of Macklin. When Hawthorn noticed, at the last minute, a signal for him to enter the pits, he quickly hit his brakes to slow for pit lane. Macklin hit his brakes too, causing a dust cloud behind him. He then swerved up the track to avoid hitting the Jaguar of Hawthorn. In doing so, he put himself directly in front of Levegh who had no time to react. Levegh ran into the rear of Macklin's Austin Healy and became airborne. His car cartwheeled toward the crowd.

The track 's spectator safety barrier consisted of an earthen mound, no fencing. This mound is where Leveghs car landed after flipping through the air, losing its front axle and bonnet. The engine mounts also broke, and the engine block hurtled into the crowd, as well. The bonnet of the car is believed to have decapitated spectators that were tightly grouped together on the sidelines.

The fuel tank ruptured and ignited the bodywork of the car which contained a high content of magnesium. The lack of knowledge in fighting a magnesiun based fire made issues worse when the rescue team tried snuffing out the flames with water. This resuted in spreading the fire. Those who hadn't been injured or killed by the flying debris suffered excruciating burns from the rampant fire. The wreckage continued to burn for hours, and it is estimated that 120 people were injured from the fire alone.

Of the 83 sectators who were hit that day, some were taken to hospital still alive, but in critcal condition, only to sucumb to their injuries in the hospital. Pierre Levegh was believed to have been killed instantly.

To keep the remainder of the spectators from a massive stampede out of the track facility, potentially blocking roads and hindering the passage of ambulances to and from the facility, the race organizers decided to continue the race. John Fitch, Leveghs co-driver called a meeting of the Dailmer-Benz board of directors that night. A decision was passed to pull out of the race in respect for the victims. The senstive nature of German cars in a French race only a decade after the end of the war was a main reason for the pull out.

The race was won by Hawthorn and his teammate Buen. Funeral services for the deceased were held the next day. The French media published pictures of Hawthorn and Buen's victory celebrations, and many found the coverage to be out of taste given to the tragedy that had taken place.
Blame for the accident was soon sought out, and an inquiry into the crash took place. The results of the inquiry found Jaguar was not responsible for the accident and the deaths that day were the result of poor and inadequate safety standards pertaining to the design of the track. This ruling resulted in bans on racing in many countries including France, Spain, Switzerland, and Germany until saftey issues at those countries tracks could be addressed and fixed.

The season continued, although on a limited schedule due to the cancellation of many of the European races and Juan Manuel Fangio takes the World Championship. Upon season ending, Mercedes Benz decides to pull out of racing.

The 1956 season didn't fare much better with the amount of races run. A blockade of the Suez Canal meant that fuel shortages in Britain and France. This pushed the season into the next year. Fangio also wins the World Championship that year, but there is a notibly decreased fan base of the sport.

In 1958, the Championship for Constructors was introduced using a point allocation for the first six cars. Eight points for 1st place, six for 2nd place, four for 3rd place, three for 4th place, two for 5th place, and one for 6th place. Unlike the drivers portion of the championship, the Constructor's Championship didn't allocate a point for fastest lap. These points were further awarded by car make. If the first and second place cars were of the same make, that constructor would recieve only 8 points, and third place would be awarded 6 points.

The 1958 Drivers Championship and the Constructors Championship were won that year under strange circumstances. The Drivers Champion was won by the flamboyant Mike Hawthorn, securing the title by only one point over Sterling Moss. Moss, affectionately known as 'Mr. Motor Racing,' was a man who held close the ideal of sportsmanship. Ironically, this ideal was what cost him the title.

During the Portugese Grand Prix earlier in the season, Hawthorn was looking at a disqualification for driving in the wrong direction while trying to restart his car after a spin. Sterling, a true man of valor, argued on Hawthorns behalf, convincing the Federation not to disqualify. The points Hawthorn recieved for that race, turned out to make the difference in points between he and Moss for the Championship. Met with the bittersweet loss, Stirling Moss, always the gentleman, took the loss with pride.

This was a pivitol season in Formula One. The ruling to change fuel to AvGas from the tradition alcohol fuel is extended to the end of the 1960 race season, and the lengths of the championship events were cut from 500 kms(three hours) to 300 kms (two hours). This season was the last for driving great Juan Manual Fangio. He retired after the French Grand Prix in Reims. It was also a year that saw three more race drivers die at events. Luigi Musso was killed at the French Grand Prix when his Ferrari crashed; Peter Collins died at the German grand Prix, also driving a Ferrari when it crashes into a tree, and Stuart Lewis-Evans succumbed to his injuries and burns after crashing at the Grand Prix of Morroco.

Mike Hawthorn retired from racing in 1958, the same year his biography "Challenge me the Race." Macklin, who had escaped the LeMans race uninjured, was surprised at Hawthorn's inadvertant claim in his book that Macklin was to blame for the accident. Even though its not directly stated in the book, Macklin still launched libel suit against Hawthorn. In 1959, Mike Hawthorn was killed in a car crash on the Guilford Interchange and the libel suit was never resolved.

As the 1950's let way to the 1960's, car builders took into account design modifation and driver safety. This included new rules and regulations that were the begining of track and car safety for years to come.

CHAPTER 3: TECHNOLOGY ADVANCES

The 1960's proved to be a significant leap forward for Formula One racing. The new rear engine cars were dominating the track. As well as the new engine position, the cars now had an aluminum sheet 'monocoque' chasis developed by Colin Chapman, lead designer at Lotus. This was a big change from the orginal chasis. The monocoque chasis was a single shell containing structural support through its external skin somewhat like an eggshell. Later, in the seventies, John Baird would go on to produce these chasis using carbon fibre because aluminum proved not to be to flexable.

Since carbon fibre is an non-isotrope material, it is one that can only be worked with by the most highly trained individuals. With carbon fibre, all the fibres must point in the same direction of the force line, giving it the sturdy quality. If the fibres do not, then the opposite will happen as with copper and aluminum. This is why the early composite materials using aluminum were combined with wood. Wood is a non-isotropic material and held the aluminun sturdy. Changing the material was a move to make cars safer for the driver but it was a process that would take years to perfect.

The FIA introduced a number of safety changes to both cars and tracks thorough this decade. Roll over bars were introduced in 1961 as a means of keeping the driver safe, and changes to the cockpit so drivers can get out easier were brought in by 1963. Fireproof suits and full face, visor covered helmets were designated mandatory, along with new fuel tanks for vehicle fire safety. This same year, FIA assumed the responsibility of track safety and introduced flag signals.

Although these new regulations were put into place, adherance to them was a slow process. It wasn't until 1968 that the first driver to actually wear a full visor helmet. It was during the practice of the British Grand Prix and that driver was Dan Gurney.

One of the great innovations of the 1960's was the introduction of composite materials invented by car designer Robin Herd. Herd was an aircraft engineer working for the Royal Aircraft Establishment when he was brought onto staff by McLaren in 1965. He built a test car using an aerospace material consisting of an aluminum and plywood combination. Initially there was some uncertanty with this new material, Some believed it wouldn't be rigid enough to protect the driver.

Jack Brabham's Repco V8 was another hit. The Repco V8 was first brought to the track in 1966. The original idea was taken from an Oldsmobile motor out of a Buick passenger car. It worked well against the other 3 litre engined cars of the mid-1960's. The car was lightweight with a spaceframe chassis and burned less fuel than the competitor, giving Brabham the advantage on the track when it came to handling, much to the surprise of those who believed the new 3 litre era would be dominated by Ferrari's V12 motor. The new regulation for 3 lts happened mid-season. It was Brabham who was the only team ready to race in a car under the new regulations.

Jack, known as 'Black Jack around the track has worn many hats in his career – driver, owner, constructor, and shrewd businessman. He was dedicated, determined and above all mechanically minded, which in Formula One was a trait that separated the boys from the men. He began in the sport in 1955, at age 29, driving John Cooper's Cooper Climax. By 1962, he had partnered with Tauranac and Motor Racing Developements was born. Together they began producing dozens of cars every year, but not for Formula One racing. He was also the only person to win a race with a car that bore his own name.

Jacky Stewart became an advocate for safety after his crash at Spa in 1966. It was the worst crash of Stewarts entire career and one that brought new light to the dangers of the sport. Stewart's life was saved by fellow drivers Graham Hill and Bob Boandurant, after his car had careened off the track. Boandurants car had also left the track but did not crash. Stewart's fuel cell had ruptured soaking him with fuel. A single spark would have engulfed him in flames. The two men pulled him out of the wreckage without thinking about the danger to themselves. Realizing how lucky he had been, Stewart began to inact change.

In 1968, Jim Clark was killed while running in a Formula 2 race in Germany. His death sparked a campaigne like no other, calling for tighter safety regulations in the sport. Due to the amount of deaths to that date drivers, boycotted the Belgian Grand prix at Spa – Francorchamps and the Nurburging in Gemany, a dangereous track known for its deadly turns.

Total deaths in the sport between 1960 and 1973 totaled 87. Some of the more well known drivers of that era included 22 year old Chris Bristow at Spa in 1960. That same race only two laps later, Alan Stacey crashed and caught fire.

In 1961 Wolfgang Von Trips was thrown from his car after a collision with Jim Clark in Italy, in 1962 Ricardo Rodriguez died at the inaugeral grand prix in Mexico and Gary Hocking was killed in a crash during practice in South Africa. In 1964 and also in 1966 the infamous Nurburgring track in Germany took two more men. Carel Godin de Beaufort was thrown from his Porche and died of his injuries after three days in hospital and John Taylor was badly burned after a crash with Jacky Ickx and also died in hospital days after the crash. Another crash of the 1964 season saw the only driver to win a championship after his death. Jochen Rindt crashed his car, a Lotus 72, during practice for the Italian Grand Prix. Since no other driver had been able to catch him in points, he was honored with the title postumously.

The loss of life during that decade brought to light the need for even more saftey regulations. While wider tires and increased downforce worked for handling, fire safety was a forefront issue. In 1969, the cars were equipped with two fire extinguishers. Yet the push to make cars safer moving into the next decade proved twice as hard for FIA thanks to the creative genius of car designers.

CHAPTER 4: THE CORPORATE MONEY OF SPONSORSHIP

Sponsorship is the financial backing of major companies and corporations in the return for their logo and company colors to be painted on the car. It has literally become the backbone of the sport since the pull out of automobile related company backing. Not always a decision agreed with by some who believed sponsorship would turn the landscape of

F1 into a consumerist's paradise and lose the image of the sport. Sponsorship has grown into the way of life for Formula One teams and their survival.

In the beginning, some of the main corporate sponsors were tobacco companies. In 1968, Lotus was sponsored by Imperial Tobacco's Gold Leaf brand. The Lotus cars were painted with the color scheme of that company: red, white, and gold. John Player's and Marlboro also sponsored cars; Mario Andretti, who also drove for Lotus, had the black of Player's, giving his car its name: 'the Black Beauty'. The BRM cars were painted the red and white of Marlboro.

In 1974 Player's had considered pulling out of Formula One altogether. One of the reasons was the poor performance of Lotus, the team they sposored. A story was run in an October issue of the Daily Press, rumoring of Player's exit, but the company hadn't made the final decision to leave until just prior to the start of the 1975 season. Player's was eventually convinced to stay on in F1, but they only granted Lotus a limited budget deal.

These sponsors infused the teams with cash, allowing them to not only race, but also construct and design better and faster cars, so Player's decision was paramount to the teams survival. Sponsoship is a business agreement, and like the ever changing drivers in the racing seat, sponsors also changed, dependant on the business commitment of the team and whether it got fulfilled or not. Some other well known sponsors of Formula One over the years since sponsorship was permitted have been Petronas, Telefonica, Panasonic, and Parmalat.

The liveries where the cars were kept and shown off have changed immensely over the years. In the beginning, the drivers waited around in the garage area. Some assisted mechanics, others sat on a pile of tires and ate a snack. Fans wandered around freely and chatted with their favorite drivers. The flag in the livery above there garage area was that driver or builder's country flag.

With sponsorship, the flags that flew became the logo of the main sponsor of that team. The pit area soon became a secured facility where passes need to be purchased and shown in order to gain access to the drivers and cars. Strict rules on who could go where were written up and enforced.

Sponsors used the cars, and the livery as their own personal ad space and each new season brought new colors to the livery, different flags of new sponsors, or changed colours of old sponsors. Most of the changes in the livery could be seen on the cars colour schemes, sometimes differing from one race to another depending on what the sponsor wanted.

With the shift in society views about tobacco, many countries by the 1990's had banned smoking in public areas. Some of the major sponsors in Formula One, the tobacco companies, were banned from advertising. In some countries, where the ban on smoking was in effect, these sponsors got around the ban by changing their liveries to reflect that situation, only flying colours instead of cigarette brand logos, repainting cars with company colours and leaving the logo off.

These changes in the livery were also seen with alcohol sposors, as well. Races that were put on by non-alcholol sponsors saw teams with alcohol sponsors like Anheiser Busch who change their advertising logo to BUD.

The countries that banned smoking actually made it difficult for major tobacco sponsors, but they had the big money, and teams did not want to lose the cash infusion, so the team and sponsor worked together to conform to the rules of those countries. Some tobacco companies are permitted, as long as they make no inference to smoking. The only tobacco sponsor banned from every host country is

Marlboro. When historical events take place, FIA allows liveries and cars to have their original sponsor colours no matter what the sponsor was at that time.

Red Bull, a major sponsor in the new millenium has gone from being a financial backer to a team owner. In 2005, they purchased Jaguar Racing and then Minardi, choosing to run the later team as an independent company.

With the knowledge of health risks from tobacco, a new controversy has unfolded on the sponsorship playing field that has doctors in an uproar. Marlboro is at the center of the controversy. The cars that they sponsor are adorned with a red, white and black barcode which doctors are say is a subliminal message because the barcode resembles the bottom of the Marlboro cigrette package.
At present, it appears to only be Ferrari, who is backed by Philip Morris, the parent company of Marlboro cigarettes, openly accepting funds from tobacco. It is an estimated $100 million deal that Ferrari does not want to lose, and, since it is the parent company with the sponsorship, not the tobacco company, there are no rules being broken.

Sponsorship has evolved into creative ad campaignes that can be almost as competitive as the

drivers and teams they sponsor. In a time of technological pursuits and where multi-million dollar
deals are the norm, Formula One has opened the
door for commercial enterprise of a sport that
started for the love of racing.

CHAPTER 5: THE RIVALRY BEGINS – FERRARI VS. MCLAREN

One of the most notable and probably the longest running feuds in the sport of Formula One would have to be that of Ferrari and McLaren. The competitive tug of war between the car makers and their drivers has spanned decades.

Ferrari was formed by Enzo Ferrari in 1948. Enzo, a streetwise businessman and former race car driver, he had been entranced by motor racing since the age of ten, when his father took him, and his brother to see a race in Bologna in 1908. He was a man with immense entrepreneurial spririt who grew up knowing it took hard work to fulfill goals. His methods garnered him the success and respect that he strived for.

Thoughout the early years of Ferrari, he groomed drivers like Alberto Ascari, Juan Manuel Fangio, Musso Castellotti, and Peter Collins, but he was a man who tended to worship his cars over the drivers. He was truly in the mind set that it was the car that one races and the driver was the tool to get it to the finish line.

In the 1970's the competitve edge was an equal push between the two car makers, McLaren winning the Constructor's Championship in 1974, then Ferrari in 1975, then back to McLaren in 1976. From then it was Ferrari dominating while McLaren worked out their design hick-ups and tried to get back on track with a new car during a pivotol turning point in F1.

For the most part, the rivalry between these two teams tended to center around the rivalries of its drivers, and in doing so, brought the rest of the team along for the ride. Being the best was the goal of all and some drivers wanted to be on the podium so badly, they would do anything to get there. And so the push continued.

The reasons behind this push and pull of the two rivalry car buiders was exacerbated by a few drivers. Ferrari had Niki Lauda, a cool calculated driver who earned the name 'the computer' because of his style. Niki started in the sport driving for BRM but moved to Ferrari in 1974 when Enzo Ferrari bought out his contract. The following year, Lauda brought home the title to Ferrari. In 1976, Niki's accident at the German Grand Prix was a tragic hit to both driver and team. He suffered 1st to 3rd degree burns over the top half of his body and was even mistakenly declared dead and read his last rights. He came out of a coma 6 weeks later, and in time for the end of that season, returned to the cock pit. But the team had suffered during his time in the hospital, and it was McLaren who took the title that year. In 1977, Niki Lauda jumped ship to work for Brabham. Despite the loss, Ferrari bounced back and won again in 1979.

The early seventies were hard for the McLaren team. Bruce McLaren was into Champ Cars as much as he was into Formula One. While testing a new Can Am car at Goodwood, he ran into some trouble. His car crashed, and the head of one of the greatest car builders had died. The loss of their patriarch Bruce McLaren left the team in a state of shock. It took three years under the management of Teddy Mayer to get back in their groove. By 1973, their drivers Hulme and Reveson were starting to win races again and would go on to win 2 titles in the next four years with the help of Ron Dennis. Teddy had sold part of the McLaren team to Dennis in 1975.

Ron Dennis had his own company, Project Four Racing. Buying out the largest share of the company and taking the helm, it wasnt long before things started to turn around. Dennis is a man who doesn't allow driver ego to get in his way. He sticks to his convictions. Over the years, he has found a majority of the drivers who have worked for McLaren giving them the break they were looking for. It was Ron's genious that pulled McLaren out of its slump.

McLaren has had some immpressive drivers in their stable over the years, most notably, Emerson Fittipaldi in the 1970s. He join the team in 1974 and won the championship for McLaren that same year. The following year he came in second in championship points and left the team the following year.

His departure left the McLaren team looking for a
driver to fill his spot. They sign the young, some
say cocky, James Hunt.

Hunt was the bad boy of Formula One. His temper
and actions landed him in the papers many times,
and he only one one championship for the team.
He had become the face of Formula One, albeit not
the face that Formula One truly wanted. Hunt raced
for McLaren for 3 years, competing against friend
and rival Niki Lauda. In 1976, Hunt took the championship by mere points because of his decision at
the final race in Japan. Hunts decision to continue
racing during the rain after Lauda retired from the
race was what gained him those points. It would be
the only championship he had ever won, and two
years later in 1978, he left McLaren for team Wolf,
only to retire from racing for good later that year
for 'self preservation reasons'.

The latter part of the seventies, to the early years of
the 1980's proved difficult for McLaren. They were
caught up in the changes that took place with car
design, and fell behind the rest of the field in regards to ground effect and turbo charging. These
issues would soon become a thing of the past. In
1982, Niki Lauda, Ferrari's ex-golden boy joins
McLaren after a hiatus from the sport. Niki won the
championship for McLaren in 1984 and 1985, then

retired that same year. But McLaren would go on to dominate in 1986 with driver Alain Prost and continue that domination from 1988 to 1991, much to the disgust of their rival Ferrari.

It wasn't only the drivers who were making the rivalries well known, it was the push of the builders to make a better car than the competition. To, in essence, build the perfect winning machine. The technological advances of the seventies were put to the test as both McLaren and Ferrari built their cars and toyed with advances yet to be seen anywhere.

Ferrari, like Williams and Tyrell, tested out the use of 6 wheeled vehicles. The 312T6 had two sets of wheels at the rear of the car. In theory, this proved great for handling, but in reality it was difficult to control. They went back to the drawing board and created the four wheeled 312B3, which brought the Ferrari team to the runner up position of the Constructor's Championship. They then created the 312T which had better aerodynamics, and improved weight distribution. It became a car worth running.

McLaren had a few designs themselves. It was designer, Ralph Bellemy, who was put at the drawing board. For the 1972 season, the M19A Cosworth was unveild. It was a new kind of design encompassing aerodynamics and some other upgrades. It had a shape like a Coca Cola bottle, with a fibre glass shell and an aluminum monocoque chasis. This car did not gain them the championship, but it did put them in a points position ahead of Ferrari that year.

These cars went through the changes like the other developers, experimenting with sidepods, wings and chasis. There was the evident tug of war in the garage that there was on the track. Building the car that could out perform the competiton while meeting the ever changing regultions put in play by FIA. Some even tried to cleverly bend the rules in order to gain that advantage.

The engines in the cars were just as essential as the design. McLaren used the Ford Cosworth motors, while Ferrari had the 'boxer' engine which was a straight 12 cylinder. The 12's, straight and V were found to be useful as rear engines as their mass sat directly above road level. It proved to be a good engine and was used for eleven years in both Formula One and the company's street version sports cars.

The Cosworth DFV's were lighter than the V-12's, meaning they had better power to weight ratio. These motors had won 167 races over a twenty year span. DFV stood for Double Four Valve and was originally created in the late sixties, a design by Keith Duckworth.

While all the British F1 teams preferred the DVF, it was McLaren that truly made the engine its own. The DFV was essentilly part of the vehicles structure with load bearing arms attaching it to the frame. This made it easier for McLaren's design teams to build a car around the motor. While Ferrari was reinventing the wheel with their heavier power supplies, McLaren was retro fitting a tried and tested dependable engine.

CHAPTER 6: THE FUTURE OF RACING – WINGED CARS AND GROUND EFFECT

By mid-1970's, it had become apparent that aerodynamics were the way of the future for Formula One cars, and in the ever growing need to become faster and win more, the challenge was on to make the perfect race car. Constructors were figuring out ways to do so.

It was also a time of change with safety. The push by Jacky Stewart to make cars safer following the deaths of so many promising drivers in a short period of time had become sobering to many who tried not to think of the possible dangers of their sport.

It was a new age of car design that saw builders finding more ways to change the cars for better performance. Aerofoils were introduced in the late 1960's with Brabham, Lotus, and Ferrari experimenting. They helped the car by providing downforce for better handling. There were many styles of aerofoils, small tabs on the front sides of the nose cone, pillar mounted front and rear, and even wedge shaped or monocoque.

The use of wings and spoilers became a big part of the constructors competition with builders using them to make cars faster, and handle better in the corners at higher speeds by using ground effect. The FIA, on the other hand, were allowing the use of wings as a way to slow the cars down and make them safer. Wings redirected air flow over the vehicle and the spoilers stabilized it. The use of these two combined allowed the car to have better control at higher speeds.

Ground effect was one of the most ingenius, and in some ways dangerous discoveries of the decade. Although the origination of ground effect had been years earlier in the Chapparral Champ Car series, the idea of using ground effect on F1 cars was the brainchild of Colin Chapman.

Chapman, an englishman, born in 1928, has been called a genius, not necessarily creatively, but a man who can incorporate the genuis ideas of others into a magnificent finished product. He almost single handedly grew the Lotus team into greatness. Using the idea of ground effect from Champ cars on the Lotus 78 design, in 1976.

The bottom of the car would essentially have upside down aerofoils running the length of the chasis with grooves guiding the air flow out the back. To decrease excess air from entering under the car sidepods were added, enclosing the bottom of the car. These changes allowed the cars to have a suction or vacuum effect. The car could corner at increased speed creating the feeling equivalent to 'driving on a rail'.

Changes to the cars also meant the need to change the tires and suspension. These changes took time. The idea to use the car's own form when designing an aeodynamic car was inspired by the shape of a World War 2 bomber's inner wing.

During this time, many teams came up with their own variations on the aerodynamic, ground effect car. McLaren was slow to get stared, choosing to wait and see what the competitors were doing. From 1978 to 1980, the team struggled to build a good performing car.

Brabham was designing his ground effect car, and even introduced the 'Fan' car. The car was designed by Brabham's own Gordon Murphy. This car had a fan mounted at the back of the car near the gearbox, enclosing the chassis. The fan cooled the motor while at the same time sucked the air from under the car. This gave it aeroynamic downforce. The faster this car went, the more suction it had. At first it was laughed at, with other teams believing Brabham as joking around. It wasn't until the fan cars landed in the top two rows on the starting grid that competitors began to get upset. Drivers complained the fan was blowing debris up into their faces, and the other team's designers were adamant that it broke specific design rules even though FIA had approved the entry of the cars weeks in advance.

The Wolf team was another builder that tried their hand in designing a ground effect car. It's new concept, the WR5 was like no other. It had a short nose and rigid honeycomb sidepods. Mounted on the dashboard was the oil cooler. It's wings were supported by two side-plates. The car itself was a bit bulky, but other teams were impressed by its all over design. It was almost the perfect car that teams had been trying to create.

By 1979, French team, Ligier and the Williams team were showing off their creations. Ligier built the JS11. An innovative concept was seen on this car that had never been seen before. The sidepods resembled shark fins, with the rear portion of the pods being at equal height to the rear tire. The idea used the rotation of the rear tire to expel the excess air from under the car.

Williams FW07 was a design inspired by the Lotus 79. It was a simplisitic design, light weight and fast. It contained the perfect proportion of lag to straight line speed. It also created the right mount of cornering downforce.

With the new designs to these cars, only Brabham and Williams took the brake system and made them outboard mounted. The brakes were also all disk at the time, which was needed to effectively slow these higher speed machines.

The 1979 season was the last to see ground effect cars which were turning laps six seconds faster than regular track times. This was disconcerting to FIA and the safety standards they were trying to enforce. They placed a ban on the grooved under-carriages and regulated that only flat bottom chasis would be allowed, sparking another era of new de-signs.

CHAPTER 7: TURBO ERA

Turbo charging, like it's predecessor, supercharging, was initially introduced or the 1977 season, along with the ground effect technology. Turbo charging was considered the way of the driving future in Formula One, despite some tiny set backs. Turbo charging was a slow developmental progression. Builders like Ferrari, with their regular aspirated cars were the driving force that year.

Car maker Renault had finally re-entered the racing world after a fifteen year hiatus as a full team, although they actively built engines in that time for other race teams including Lotus. With the turbo charged RS01 that had a Gordini V6 turbo, They raced it at the British Grand Prix. Although this car was quick to accelerate, its unreliability led to a year of unfinished races.

In 1980, the newsest team in the stable who only had a season under their belt, Williams Racing, began to rise to the top. Turbo charging had finally burst out of its growing pains and Williams, with Alan Jones at the wheel, dominated. Ferrari, a once top competitor, experienced their worst season ever.

FISA brought into play new rules in 1981 regarding ground effect in order to decrease a drivers cornering speed. They banned the slidding skirt that aided the cars design and in 1982 added rules about contracted driving, which did not allow drivers to get in the seat of anothers car. They had to race for who they were contracted to. This was an issue that struck a cord with drivers Niki Lauda and Didier Pironi and the two drivers arranged a walk out for the South African Grand Prix.

In 1983, driving a turbo charged BMW, Piquet won his second championship. The turbo era was in full bloom, and everyone seemed to want in the garden.

That year, McLaren unveiled its new turbo charged TAG-Porsche engine, and won four races with driver Alain Prost in 1983.

It was also a year that saw a rivalry of a different kind. This rivalry was between the governing bodies of the sport. It caught media attention, splitting the drivers support and overshadowing the accomplishments of the racing world. Formula One Constructors Association (FOCA) headed by newly appointed Bernie Ecclestone and (FISA) head Jean-Marie Balestre disagreed on the limitations of ground effect. Ecclestone argued that unrestricted ground effect would even out the field, whilst Balstre was quick to argue that restricting the ground effect was safer. In the end, it was FOCA who won the disagreement and unrestricted ground effect was how the drivers ran.

One of the top car designers of the eighties was Rory Byrne, an acclaimed South African engineer best known for designing the winning cars of Ferrari and Benetton. He joined the Formula One world in 1981 after working with Toleman on designing Formula Two chasis.

Through the eighties, rivalries amongst the builders and the drivers heated up the Formula One racing scene. The turbo era continued with many noteworthy wins. Nigel Mansell's first place finish at Brands Hatch for Renault, Niki Lauda's 5 wins, Provsts 7 wins. And, Ayrton Senna, in a car owned by Toleman, in his inaugural season, passed Prost on the last lap of the 1984 Monaco Grand prix. Race officials had called the race due to rain. Despite Senna having passed Prost, it was Prost that was given the win. That started a rivalry that would go on for years.

This was also the year McLaren began to dominate the track with their TAG motor. Some critics believe McLaren's dominance was sheer luck, but the new car designed by John Barnard, the MP4/2 was a powerhouse and became a sign of change on and off the track.
With the power of the turbo engines, the cars needed to be modified to keep them on the track. Some teams built sliding skirts along the bottom of the sidepods to help increase ground effect and downforce to keep the cars on the track but safety issues ensued and FIA brought in the rules against sliding skirts. The rule clearly stated "at any time all suspended parts of the car must be no less than 6cm from the ground." This rule sent desingers back to the drawing board in an attempt to meet regulations.

Jack Braham's team came up with a unique and controversial solution that defied the rule but technically did not break it. They designed the hydaulic suspension. While stationary, the car conformed to the rule, but on the track, at speed, the car would lower. This design meant the cars were actually suspensionless. That posed two serious probems. The first was the drivers worried the cars may lose ground effect on the chicanes and would be harder to control. The second was the bottom of the chasis rubbing on the pavement and cracking the shell. The solution to that problem was to line the bottom edge of the chasis with a special rubbing strip.

The progression of the turbo era was quite slow. The first engines developed and used in racing suffered from turbo lag, meaning they took some time to get going during exceleration. This was an issue on the track, where getting up to speed was important.

By the end of the 1980's, turbo charging and the turbo era days were numbered. The final year of the turbo engine was 1988 and an era that started the same time as ground effect, soon saw the same demise. In 1989, FIA mandated that only normally aspirated engines could be run.

F1

CHAPTER 8: A NEW RIVALRY – MCLAREN- WILLIAMS

The rivalry between Ferrari and McLaren was slowly fading with the rise of the other competitor Williams. Sir FrankWilliams' team had worked hard to make it into the ranks with Ferrari and McLaren, who gave the latter a real run for the title.

Williams got onto racing during the 1960's as a driver in Formula Three, then was team manager in Formula Two. In 1969, he had started in Formula One, albeit with a tight pocket book and a few chuckles from competitors in the garage. It took financial backing from a source in the Middle East and the joining of forces with Patrick Head, an engineer, to actually get the company off the ground. When they did, they no longer were the laughing stock, but true contenders looking for the title.

Between 1980 and 1997 Williams had won the Constructor's Championship nine times. The 1986 win with their FW11 was the only season where the field was made up of all turbo charged engined cars. It was also the same year McLaren driver Alain Prost won the Drivers Championship. Throughout the eighties, drivers Nigel Mansell and Nelson Piquet were the drivers that put Williams on top.

Changes in the Formula in 1987, bringing back the atmospheric motors and allowing 3.5 lt capacity engines, as well as restricting the turbo engines boost pressure and fuel capacity could be seen as a leg up for McLaren. In the 1988 season, it was the McLaren team who dominated, winning 15 of the 16 races between their two drivers, Alain Prost and Ayrton Senna.

McLaren's dominance was in effect for three more seasons, and no doubt the reason behind this was the slowly inflating rivalry of the teams two drivers. It was a push for dominance between the two that saw McLaren on the podium race after race.

Yet this rivalry could also be seen as the car builders downside and weak point. The rivarly of Prost and Senna was a public affair on and off the track. At the Suzuka Grand Prix in Japan in 1990, the two drivers crashed while racing for contention.. Prost said he was 'closing the door on him', but Ayrton Senna openly admitted to running directly into his team mate.

While McLaren was busy winning championships and refueling their drivers, Williams was working on becoming a dominating force once again. They had switched to Renault power under the hood. This change, along with the regulatory changes made by FIA, aided in the Williams team to re-take the podium for the next seven years. Memorable wins in those years included Nigel Mansell in 1992. He achieved his first drivers title after a decade of trying. Alain Prost, caputured his fourth title in 1993.

In 1994, Senna left McLaren to drive for Williams. It was that same year that Williams partnered with

Mercedes on an engine deal. Only three races into the season, Ayrton Senna lost his life at Imola in the San Marino Grand Prix when his car shot directly at the Tamburello's corner and hit the wall. It happened on the second lap after a restart.

Although the true cause of Sennas crash has never been determined, both head engineers were aquitted of all neglegence charges at both the court trial and the appeal. On board computers show Senna let off the throttle, but that was not enough to correct the car. The loss of downforce from driving over the chicane may have been a factor.

The remainder of the season proved unsucessful for team Williams. It was Benetton who won the Conctructors Championship in 1995 by Michael Schumacher who was driving for that team. The following year he moved to Ferrari and the era of Michael Schumacher arrived.

Williams recovered from their loss of Senna and won the 1996 Constructors Championship, but it was in 1998 that the the Willims-McLaren rivalry heated up again. Designer Adrian Newey had jumped ship from Williams to McLaren and desined his new team a car that was like no other. The Mp4-13 took Haikkenen to the podium eight

times that year and he was named Driver Champion.
McLaren also won their first Constructors Championship in 7 years.

With Schumacher at Ferrari, and McLaren doing
well, the latter part of the 1990's were not fairing so
well with Williams. Despite having the talented
Jaques Villeneuve in their stable, they could only
break third place..

As the new millenium arrived, it was a push in a
different direction. By 2005, Williams and engine
suplier BMW had a volitile parting of ways. Switch-
ing to non-works Cosworth engines the following
year appeared to be a posititve move, but result
were not as planned.

Times were changing, and it appeared the old
wound between builders would be re-opened.
McLaren showed much promise and Ferrari was
right up there to match them, leaving third place,
Williams, fighting to keep up. The era of the
Williams-McLaren rivalry had finally turned.

CHAPTER 9: SAFETY REGULATIONS

Some of the Williams dominance was attributed to the regulatory changes and design. FIA brought back mandatory fueling, a rule that had not been seen in years. In doing this, teams were forced to re-stratgize how they ran the races. Teams also began to introduce their own electronic driving aids. Lotus designed the active suspension, Ferrari brought in the semi-automatic gear boxes, and Williams presented traction control.

These new adaptations were, from the builders stand point, to make the cars faster. That, in turn made racing more dangerous, so FIA stepped in and placed bans on certain driver aids they deemed dangerous, but the inability to properly police such bans, however, made it difficult and many teams got away with breaking the rules.

Eight years of rule changes between 1986 and 1994 had proven positive. There had been no deaths from any on-track crashes. This, however, was more of an illusion of safety. The dark cloak of death would be worn again at the May race of the San Marino Grand Prix, and again, two weeks later at Monaco.

The entire May 1st weekend was marred with tragedy. Rubens Borrichetto was seriously injured in an accident during Friday practice, Roland Ratzenburger crashed during qualifying; and the 3 time World Champion, Ayrton Senna died as a result of a crash during the race. Both Ratzenburg and Senna died of injuries to their heads, Ratzenburg of a basal skull fracture, and Senna of severe head trauma. As the wreckge of Senna's car was being examined, they found a furled Austrian flag the Senna had planned on waving in honor of his friend Roland Ratzenburger.

As the racing world mounred, two weeks after the dark May weekend, Karl Wendlinger, a driver for team Sauber crashed at Monaco and was in a coma for 19 days. He tried to get back into Formula One but found he couldn't compete. He went on to drive touring cars for Audi.

FIA jumped into action, pushing for even more safety, forcing changes. It began with the limiting of air intake to reduce engine power. Then in 1995, the first design templates were brought to Formula One. Other legs of racing had been using templates for years, now the builder's free reign on car design in F1 had come to an end. With this design template, all cars had to conform to a specific design which had strict limits. Cockpit size, wing height, and vehicle shape were all part of the new regulatory design. Engine restrictions were also brought into effect, allowing only 3 litre engines, as opposed to 3.5 litre.

Tires were also changed. The introduction of grooved tires replaced the slick tires of years gone by. These new tires were meant to reduce speeds in cornering by causing slip so that the drivers had to let off the throttle to control their cars.

Strict adherance to the rules were conducted by FIA through rigorous tests to check for proper wing height, stiffness and regulatory measurements. Wind tunnels were becoming used more and more in both design and policing.

CHAPTER 10: DEMISE OF THE PRIVATEERS

Privateers are what the smaller independant run teams were called. At one time, that was what the sport was made up of. Now these pioneers of racing have gone extinct. Big corporate conglomerates rule the landscape of Formula One.

Back in the day, privateers were a common sight. In 1961, Giancarlo Baghetti won his first race driving

privately owned Ferrari. No other driver has ever
won won their first race.

Before arriving in the ranks of Formula One, mosts
teams get their experience racing other Formulae
or even other types and classes of racing like
Sauber, who was a winner of both LeMans and
World Sports Car series.

Team Sauber was an independent team from
Switzerland. The rein holder of this outfit was Peter Sauber. A quiet, focused Swiss man who rarely
likes to speak english, Peter began building cars in
1970. His team ran competitively for over decade.
They always showed consistent finishes against the
big name teams. Stauber was also willing to work
with manufacturers, namely Mercedes and Ferrari.
He is a bit of a private man, not media hungry like
his counterparts on other teams. Even the team
sponsors were low key. In 2006, this unassuming
patriarch handed his team to BMW changing the
name to BMW Sauber and the new team head became Mario Theissen. Peter Sauber's privateering
days had ended.

The Forti team created by Italian egineer Paolo
Guerci and former Italian race car driver Guido
Forti started of in the 1970s in the smaller Formula
Three series. It was the finacial backing of Brazilian

driver Pedro Diniz in 1995 that gave the Forti team the finacial boost to make it into the Formula One. Yet, even with the financial backing, they struggled to make it. Those were the risk privateers took. And it was a gamble for those willing to put up money for a private team to run, but Diniz had his own agenda. He wanted to form an all-Brazilian team, giving his son, Pedro the reins of the team's main car. As good as this sounded, the results were not great. Neither Pedro, or Robetto Moreno, the other driver for the team, managed to fair well. The team became the laughing stock of the garage area.

They all had good intentions, and grand dreams, but sometimes plans didn't work out. Unfortunately with Forti, they slowly fell into debt and could not fight their way out.

As other independent teams dwindled out of existence, it saw the brains and bonze of the sport dwindle away also. Throughout the late eighties and into the nineties, the corporate shift was taking place. Only teams with conviction to continue privatering fought. Minardi, Jack Brabham, Ken Tyrell, Colin Chapman, and Bernie Ecclestone. These men spent blood sweat and motor oil to build their teams. At that time, it was the only way to do things. But with the cash backing of corporate sponsors and the dwindling funds of the independent, the landscape changed.

In 1987, Renault disbanded their racing team, but continued to be part of Formula One by building engines for the other teams. Not long after, the French team Legier left. The Jordan team lingered for a couple more seasons, only to sell out. Even the great Benetton closed its doors when finances became tight. Some may chalk it up as the growing pains of Formula One, but in reality it was a slow painful take over with financial backing being the key.

By 2004, Ford Motor company pulled out of Formula One leaving the remaining smaller run companies wounded. These smaller teams depended on the Ford motors. Without their main engine supplier, they didn't have cars to race. Jaguar sold to Red Bull and in 2005 and was rebranded as the Red Bull Racing.

Minardi, run by Paul Stoddard, continuously fought against the ever changing tide. He watched those around him disapear behind corporation bank rolls. He constantly fought to keep his team on top, only to faulter in the end. Minardi was the last privateering company to sell out as the corporate struggle between David and Goliath saw David crumble forever. A team that was formed on 1980 by Gian-carlo Minardi, who began by running cars in for-mula two. Nine years later, the Minardi team was in the top ten, a great feat for a small team. Twelve years later, Australian, Paul Stoddard, a privateer in his own right, bought the majority share of the Mi-nardi company and continued to run it under the legenday Minardi name. When the end came with the sale of Minardi to Red Bull, it was for the job security of his staff that he handed the hat over to Detrich Mateschitz, owner of red bull. The Minardi name now Scuderia Toro Roso the team is as an independent entity from Red Bull, although its liv-ery bradishes the Red Bull colors.

With the end of the last great privateer, the new age of corporate racing began. Occasionally there may be inedependents brave enough to try to run up against the line up of goliaths, yet without the major financial backing, an attempt is all it will be.

CHAPTER 11: FERRARI'S GOLDENBOY – MICHAEL SCHUMACHER

By 2000 Michael Schumacher was Ferrari's golden-boy. He brought back the World Championship to the car maker for the first time in two decades. The last time that Ferrari had seen the coveted title was in 1979 when Jody Schecker had won it.

By 1999, the car builder had the perfect super team consisting of Schumacher; Jean Todt, team manager; technical director. Ross Brawn; and engine designer Rory Byrne. Their efforts were what aided the rise of Ferrari into the new era.

Throughout the early part of the new millenia, Ferrari dominated the ranks as the last few remaining privateers closed their doors for good. Yet, with that dominance, the team became less liked by the fans.

The antics of the car builder were part of the blame for this shift in fan base support. They had been accused of staging finishes at the Australian Grand Prix and the US grand Prix. The FIA even went ahead and made some changes to the rules in order to end the dominance of teams and even out the playing field, but that, unfortunately, wasn't going to be enough. Michael Schumacher won the title once again.

Michael Schumacher, born in Germany in 1969 got his start in racing in Kart. It was Willi Webber, manger to many German race drivers, who moved him from small time to formula racing, starting the young Schumacher in cars and then in Formula Three. He showed immense promise as a race car driver and in 1990, after winning the German

Championship, the Jordan team brought him into Formula One. He made his debut for them in 1991, only to be traded to Benetton later that year.

Michael joined Ferrari in 1996, when he was 27. He hadjust won his first championship. His methods for winning some may call calculated risk while others may say was pure selfishness. In order to guarantee the title he took out both Damon Hill and himself, so the Hill would not gain the points on him to win.

Despite his unconventional methods, it is Michael's driving ability that sets him apart from most drivers. Where Ayrton Senna came close to his idea of perfection, Michael Schumacher has epitomized it, surpassing every bar put in front of him. Michael has won a total of 7 championships in his career, started 308 races and garnered 1566 points.

Schumacher matched racing great Fangios record of five Driver's Championships in 2003. The fifth was a difficult win as the change to the point recording had teams racing right to the last track of the season. He by-passed the that record the following year with a miraculous sixth title win. By 2004, it appeared it was all-Michael, all the time. Schumacher won 13 times that season and took the Championship for the seventh time.

2006 was a lousy year for both car maker and driver. The tire manufacturer was now Bridgestone and the Ferrari cars were not running well on those tires. Their main driver had difficulty too, only winning seven races.

That was the year that Michael Schumacher decided to retire. He had brought Ferrari to the top, with the help of the unbeatable team of Schumacher-Todt-Brawn-Byrne. Together they were a combination of driving force, technical know how, engineering genious and flawless design.

Michaels retirement was a bitter sweet time for Ferrari. With Michael's help, the Ferrari team reached greatness in the 21st century, but to see if they could sustain greatnes, it was left up to them. Technical director Ross Brawn also took a leave of absence as his faith was waivering on the changes going on in the Ferrari coral. The next one to fill the great driver's shoes was talented Kimi Raikkonen, teaming up with Felipe Massa behind the wheel of the other Ferrari car.

CHAPTER 12: FERRARI-GATE – RETURN OF THE RIVALRY

With Ferrari's dominance in the early part of the new millenium, McLaren and Williams having suffered set backs, slowly began to fade out of sight. By 2005, Ferrari's heyday had come and gone as

Renault, rose to contention with driver Fernando Alonso.

The latter part of that season saw McLaren fight back to become real competition for Renault. That year also saw the shift for Williams as they ended their relationship with BMW and joined forces with Cosworth. To add to the major shift on the track, FIA brought an end to the use of the V10 engine, replacing it with the 2.4Lt. V8 engines.

With Michael Schumacher gone, and Kimi Raikkonen, former McLaren driver at Ferrari, the two car makers opened old wounds and the rivalry of the new era began. Ferrari had been accused of staging races in the past and McLaren had lost their best driver to the other team. The actions causing headlines next were almost unbelievable.

2007 was the year best known for the biggest case of corporate espionage in the history of Formula One. Even though it was a case of the employees hatching the plans, ultimately it was the companies themselves being punished. McLaren had been caught in the possession of design schematics from the Ferrari stable. The issue known as Spy-gate, Ferrari-gate and Stepney-gate became world news.

It was like something straight from a spy movie, involving four race teams, and many players. This espionage story began with a disgruntaled Ferrari employee Nigel Stepany and a senior engineer at McLaren, Mike Coughlan.

Mid-2007 Stepany approached Coughlan with a 780 page design dosier from Ferrari. Around that same time, both men had approached Honda F1 inquiring about positions within that company. Coughlan's wife, Trudy, took the dosier to a local Woking print shop to have it burnt onto cds. Woking, is the homebase of McLaren. An employee of the shop thought something was out of sorts when he saw the Ferrari logo on the material and contacted them by email regarding the material Trudy Coughlan had brought in. The cat was out of the bag. Trudy picked up the two cds the next day and returned home to shred and burn the dosier, as her husband had instructed.

Over the next few months, an investigation ensued. It included the Italian police and high court. Nigel Stepany is released from his duties at Ferrari, and initially Mike Coughlan was suspended from McLaren, but was later fired for his role in the matter and given a two year ban from Formula One racing.

In July, the FIA had a hearing, but no penalties resulted for McLaren. A second hearing in September of that year with new evidence being presented resulted in several penalties for McLaren, the worst being the exclusion of the team from the Constructor's Championship that year and a whopping 100 million dollar fine.

A few months later, It was McLaren who approached the FIA in regards to allegations that the Renault F1 team was in possession of their 2006/2007 car designs. Renault was found guilty, but were not punished.

In 2009 legal proceedings were dropped against the accused parties but resulted in fines for Mike Coughlan (€180,000) Paddy Lewis, Jonathan Neale, and Rob Taylor (€150 000 each).

Five years on and the repercussions of the biggest punishment in F1 history still lingers. McLaren, prooving that racing is just as much about business as it is about the sport have won the right to claim 32 million pounds of their FIA penalty as a tax deductable. This cost would be reflected against their corporation tax, saving them millions of dollars.

The fight to get this deduction was seen before a government tribunal who came to the final decion in McLarens favor, backing up the teams stance that paying penlties is all part of doing business.

With his two year ban served, Mike Coughlan is now back in the racing world, hired on by Williams. Nigel Stepany is now team manager at FIA GT1 World Championship where he has been since 2010. September 29, 2010 he was found guilty of sabotage, industrial espionage, sporting fraud and attempting serious injury for his role in the Spygate scandle. His sentance was twenty months in jail an €600, but it is unlikely he will serve the jail time under the Italian legal system.

CONCLUSION: 21ST CENTURY AND BEYOND

At the beginning of the 21st century, many changes began to happen. Crash testing impact speeds were increased to 14 metres per second, and the roll bar height was increased by 20cms. There was the also an increase to the thickness of the carbon fibre walls which had to be at least 3.5mm thick and a kevlar layer inside the cockpit wall of 2.5mm is added for extra resistence to penetration.

Technological advances have allowed for many new changes in how FIA allows pit crews to fix cars. Two way tilemtry was allowed in 2002, so now pit technicians not only recieve information from the cars computer components, but they are also allowed to re-adjust remotely without he need for cars to pit.

Driver apparell has changed tremendously over the years, from open faced helmets to full faced helmets, and fire suit technology increasing over the decades. But when it comes to driver saftey, the Hans device, introduced into the sport in 2003 was a pivotal decision.

Despite the rules of higher and thicker cock pit walls, the drivers could still receive heavy head injuries at impact speed from their heads moving around. The hans device, designed by the US company Head and Neck Protection Systems is a horseshoe shaped device that rests on the drivers shoulders. It is attached to the six point safety harness and the rear of the helmet. Helmets can weigh up to 7.5 kg, and a driver can experience over 100 g's during an impact causing severe head and neck trauma. The Hans device reduces the weght on a drivers neck, holding it in place during impact.

Track rules for safety have been a prominent issue in the past. Marshalls are now protected by stricter safety specifications, the blue flag rule imposes a 10 second stop and go penalty if a driver, by the third waving of the flag, does not let the car behind him pass when that flag is shown. Stop and go penalties are also imposed for other rule breaking, as well. False starts causing accidents and forcing other drivers off the track are all enforced with these penalties.

Many tracks have undergone facelifts in order to make them safer..Silverstone gets new asphalt on the Stowes corner runoff zone, Nurburgring revised its chicane before the last corner, Magny-Cours has a new exit lane, allowing for cars to return onto the track at full speed, Budapest and Suzuka have larger run off zones. Monty Carlo is even upgraded with a permanent pit lane and garage area. But the safest track in Formula One, and probably the most modern, is the Istanbul Park Circuit that is used for the Turkish Grand prix.

The landscape of Formula One has changed immensely over 60 plus years. The cars have gotten faster, the drivers more self aware, and Teams more financially dependant on the mighty dollars of the corporate conglomerates. The one change that has taken place and will continue into the future is safety. From the cars, to the tracks, to driver apparel, Formula One continues to strive for the safest racing environment for everyone.

This is a sport that will go on for years to come. As long as there are brave men and women to get behind the wheel there will be Formula One racing.

BIBLIOGRAPHY

Incandela, Sal; The Anatomy and Development of the Formula One Racing Car from 1975; Somerset, England; 1990

Grant-Brabham, Bruce; Lotus. A Formula One Team History; Wiltshire, UK; 1994

Jones, Bruce; The Complete Encyclopedia of Formula One ; London, UK; 2007

Arron, Simon and Hughs, Mark; The Complete Book of Formula One; Minneapolis, MN, USA; 2008

Norton, Alex; The rivalries that make F1; www.portalf1.com

Drew, Richard; Corporates triumph ver provateers and F1 the poorer for it; posted 06 July, 2005; http://www.scmp.com

Manishin, Glenn B.; The Turbo Era; posted 1997; http://f1-grandprix.com

Author unknown; the Seventies, the eighties; www.atlasf1.com

Author unknown; Safety in the 1950s and 1960s through to the 1990s and into the 21st century; F1 Official site, www.formula1.com

Rimmer, Bev; Whatever happened to the Forti team?; posted 25 January, 2013; www.formula1fancast.com

Williamson, Martin; Deaths in Formula One; posted 02 April, 2013; en.espnf1.com

Author unknown; People: Robin Herd; posted 13 November, 2013; http://www.grandprix.com

Melissen, Wouter; Brabham – BT24 ; posted 07 August, 2006; http://www.ultimatecarpage.com

Johnston, John W.; Silverstone Race Track; posted 02 April, 2013; http://www.jwjonline.net

CPSIA information can be obtained
at www.ICGtesting.com
Printed in the USA
BVOW04s0229250517

485158BV00001B/36/P

9 781629 173856